The Flowering Hawthorn

the flowering
hawthorn

BY

HUGH ROSS WILLIAMSON

ILLUSTRATED BY

Clare Leighton

HAWTHORN BOOKS, INC., *Publishers*

NEW YORK

FIRST EDITION

November, 1962

H-3712

For
Kenneth Giniger

The Flowering Hawthorn

1

A T THE END of August in the year 1535, Thomas Cromwell, Vicar-General to King Henry VIII, received an unexpected gift from one of his officials in the west of England. It was "two flowers, wrapped in black and white sarsnet." The flowers were hawthorn, which, so the giver explained, were from a tree in Glastonbury that "on Christen Mass Even, at the hour when Christ was born, will spring and burgeon and bear blossoms." History does not relate whether Cromwell took the hawthorn to the King, who was more concerned with preparations to destroy the Abbey of Glastonbury and take for himself its more durable properties than with the Holy Thorn which grew there on "the holiest earth in England." But there is no doubt that he knew of the giant tree, with the double trunk, which had stood on Weary-all Hill from time immemorial and would always "blossom at Christmas, mindful of Our Lord." For it was part of the tradition of England.

A poem of the Middle Ages referred to

The hawthornes also that groweth in Wirral *
Do burge and bear grene leaves at Christmas
As freshe as other in May

and only thirteen years before the gift of hawthorn to Cromwell, 'Blossoms Inn', off Cheapside—whose sign was the white blossoms of the Glastonbury Thorn—had been commandeered by the King to house the retinue of a visiting monarch.

The Hawthorn blooms still and in 1929 it was linked again with royalty when King George V accepted the gift of some Christmas flowers which, in like manner, have been offered to his successors.

In the centuries between the sixteenth and the twentieth, it has engaged the attention of botanists. First was John Gerard, in the reign of Elizabeth I, whose list of the plants in his own garden in Holborn was the first catalogue of plants, but who went further afield in his *Herball,* published in 1597, to mention: "Of the White Thorn or Haw-

* i.e. Weary-all.

[2]

thorn Tree we have in the west of England one growing at a place called Glastonbury which bringeth forth flowers about Christmas." About fifty years later, Bishop Goodman of Gloucester had to confess that he found the Thorn "very extraordinary; for, at my being there, I did consider the place—how it was sheltered. I did consider the soil and all other circumstances; and yet I could find no natural cause." A contemporary of the Bishop, John Ray, who is known as the father of natural history in England and who wrote a systematic description of plants, came to the conclusion that the Thorn differed only accidentally from the common hawthorn but his successor in botanic classification, the Cambridge professor, John Martyn, agreed that it was a distinct variety.

It was left to William Withering, the chief physician of Birmingham General Hospital (whose affection for foxgloves made him try to introduce them into the pharmacopoeia) to give the Hawthorn a distinct name. He called it *Cratagus Oxyacantha Praecox* and wrote of it: "It blossoms twice a year. The winter blooms, which are about the size of a sixpence, appear about Christmas, but sometimes sooner. These produce no fruit. The berries contain only one seed and there seemed only to have been one pistil: but it was late in the season when I examined it (October 1792). I was informed that the berries, when sown, produce plants nowise differing from the common hawthorn."

Subsequent botanists have confirmed this curious fact. Plants grown from the haws of the Glastonbury Thorn do not retain the characteristics of the parent stem and the only way it can be propagated is by grafting or budding upon other roots. Richard Gough, a contemporary of Withering, noted that the tree was common in Palestine and flowered at the same time, which led to the theory that the original Holy Thorn was brought to Glastonbury by some pilgrim from the Holy Land or, perhaps, some returning Crusader. We are on the way back to the original legend.

In 1842, John Claudius Loudon published his *Encyclopaedia of Trees and Shrubs* in which he dwelt with particular pleasure upon the Holy Thorn. "The most remarkable legend," he says, "connected with the Hawthorn is that of the Glastonbury Thorn" and in his version of it he makes St. Joseph of Arimathea arrive at Glastonbury on Christmas Day at the spot where he had been commanded by Christ to build a church in honor of the Virgin Mary. Finding that the natives were not inclined to believe in his mission, he prayed to God to perform a miracle to convince them. His prayer was at once answered and, as he struck his staff into the ground of Weary-all Hill on which he was standing to address the unbelievers, it im-

". . . it immediately shot forth into leaves and blossoms."

mediately shot forth into leaves and blossoms.

There are other forms of the legend, but they all involve Joseph of Arimathea. "We need not believe that the Glastonbury legends are records of facts," as the historian E. A. Freeman has it; "but the existence of those legends is a very great fact." And before we go back to try to discover what truth could have been in the traditional story, it is worth recording one other historical fact. In the fifteenth century, when the great Councils at Pisa and at Constance were exercised about the matter of the precedence of Bishops and Ambassadors, the English were given pride of place before the French and the Spanish on the grounds that they had first received the Gospel from the lips of Joseph of Arimathea, "who took down Christ from the Cross" and buried Him in his own tomb.

2

ONE OF THE BEST known of William Blake's poems and one which, in England, has almost attained the status of a second National Anthem is *Jerusalem* of which the first verse runs:

> And did those feet in ancient time
> Walk upon England's mountains green?
> And was the Holy Lamb of God
> On England's pleasant pastures seen?
> And did the Countenance Divine
> Shine forth upon our clouded hills?
> And was Jerusalem builded here
> Among those dark satanic mills?

The tradition to which these lines refer is that, as a boy or young man, Jesus Christ came to

England, in company with Joseph of Arimathea who was visiting the tin mines of Cornwall in which he had financial interests. Is there any reason in the nature of things why this should not have been so?

Herodotus, writing in the fifth century before Christ's birth, refers to Cornwall as "the Tin Islands" and there is evidence that the Cornish tin trade was already important to Europe even earlier—in the Late Bronze Age. It continued to flourish certainly until the beginning of the Christian era. Diodorus Siculus, a Greek historian who was a contemporary of Julius Caesar and Augustus, has actually left an account of the tin working in western Cornwall about the time of Julius Caesar's invasion of Britain in 55 B.C. The tin was mined, beaten into squares and carried in wagons to the port of Ictis, which is usually assumed to have been St. Michael's Mount. Two well-defined routes crossed Cornwall, passing directly through the important mining centers—one running from the Camel to the Fowey estuary, the other from St. Ives Bay to St. Michael's Mount. From the Cornish port, the metal was shipped across to France and carried on pack horses to Marseilles, whence it was re-exported by sea to the Mediterranean countries. The operation was highly organized, as might have been expected from the five hundred years of experience behind it. But Caesar's conquest of the Veneti and the consequent destruction of Corbilo, the port to which the tin was shipped from Ictis, was a severe blow to the prosperity of the western sea-routes and to the international character of the Cornish trade, which gradually declined. As is the way with economic changes this took time to show itself, but it would not be unfair to suppose that within sixty years or so a business man in the Eastern Mediterranean whose wealth was derived from the tin trade might think it worth his while paying a visit to Cornwall to see for himself what had gone wrong with the source of his income. Thus, if Joseph of Arimathea were such a man, it would be precisely at this time—sometime between 13 and 30 A.D.—that he might be expected to be in England to carry out his first-hand observations.

That Joseph was involved in the tin trade we have nothing but a tradition in the craft itself. This has lingered on into this century and, as one example of it, it may be worth recalling a reference in a newspaper in 1933. A visitor to the workshop of some London organ-builders was watching the metal pipes being made. To obtain a perfectly smooth and well-blended surface, a shovelful of molten metal is thrown along a table on which a linen cloth is stretched. The operation demands considerable skill. The visitor was intrigued to hear each workman, before he made his cast, saying in a low voice: "Joseph was in the tin trade." After some persuasion, he induced the foreman to explain this to him. "We workers in metal are a very old fraternity," the foreman told him, "and like other handicrafts we have our traditions. One of these is that Joseph of Arimathea, the rich man of the Gospels, made his money in the tin trade with Cornwall."

This brought a letter from a Cornish woman, whose father was a miner and who had been brought up in a mining village, to say that she remembered the carols sung by the children. One of them began: "Joseph was a merchant, a tin merchant, a tin merchant" and described his arrival from the sea in a boat.

These are but confirmations of the tradition, noted by Baring-Gould, that has been kept alive through the centuries by the tinners shouting, when the tin is flashed, "Joseph was in the trade."

Granted this possibility—for it is that precisely, no more, no less—is it at all likely that Joseph's visit would also involve Jesus as a youth? The inquiry must begin with what is actually known of Joseph from the New Testament narratives.

All four Gospels tell how, after the Crucifixion, Joseph of Arimathea, a rich councillor who was a secret disciple of Jesus and had dissented from the verdict condemning Him, went boldly to Pilate and begged that he might take away the body for burial in his own tomb. Pilate readily gave permission and Joseph, aided by another secret disciple, Nicodemus, took possession of the body, wrapped it in a clean winding-sheet, and buried it in the grave, hewn out of rock in a garden, which he had prepared for himself.

The story is so familiar that one aspect of it is usually overlooked. Jesus had been put to death by the demand of the Jewish authorities, reinforced by popular clamor and officially endorsed by the Romans. It was, in this sense, a national verdict on one who had committed the supreme blasphemy of claiming to be the Divine Messiah. In these circumstances, it would have been natural if Pilate had refused to allow the criminal to be buried anywhere but in one of the two burying places reserved for felons outside Jerusalem. At the very least it might be thought that the Roman Procurator would have consulted the Jewish Elders before giving consent to an action likely to infuriate them. Yet there seems to have been no hesitation in Pilate's granting of Joseph's immediate and bold request.

If, however, Joseph were a relation of Jesus, the proceedings would be explicable enough. Both Jewish and Roman law made it a duty for the nearest relative to dispose of the dead without any reference to the manner in which they had died. (It was this circumstance which, later, made it possible for the early Christians in Rome to claim for burial in the Catacombs the remains of those who had died in the arena.) A tradition of the Eastern Church asserts that Joseph of Arimathea was an uncle of the Virgin Mary—the younger brother of her father. Were this so, Joseph's action would not only be the natural and expected one in the circumstances, but Pilate's co-operation would arouse no antagonism among the Jews. Thus, by inference, the known Gospel lends support to what might otherwise be dismissed as an imaginative legend.

Some writers see an additional inference in the story of the twelve-year-old Jesus visiting Jerusalem for His first Passover. How did it happen that Mary and Joseph, returning home, had gone a day's journey before they noticed that He was missing "and sought Him among their kinsfolk and acquaintance," eventually returning to Jerusalem to find Him in the Temple talking with the Doctors? Arimathea—the modern Ramallah—was about eight miles north of Jerusalem and the first stopping-place for caravans traveling on the Jerusalem-Nazareth road. If Joseph of Arimathea were the Virgin Mary's uncle, it would be natural that they should stay at his house—or at least stop there on their way to the north. And, as Joseph would also be in Jerusalem for the Pass-

[14]

over, they might well have supposed that their absent Son was in his company for the first part of the return journey. It was only on their arrival at Arimathea that they found He was missing.

Whatever the validity of this suggestion, we know certainly that the Gospels are silent on the life of Jesus between the episode of the finding of Him in the Temple at the age of twelve and His baptism in Jordan at the age of thirty. The interim is the "hidden years," the events of which have been the subject of so much pious speculation. It has even been suggested that, during them, He traveled to India and became acquainted with Buddhism. But it is surely more likely, granted His relationship with Joseph of Arimathea, that He was allowed to accompany His great-uncle on a business trip and, as tradition avers, trod the fields of Cornwall.

3

Traditions of varying value—some from *Acts of Pilate* (or the *Gospel of Nicodemus*) in the apocryphal New Testament writings; some from the metrical *Life of Joseph of Arimathea,* which has origins older than the Middle Ages in which it was popular; some from the first British historian, Gildas, who wrote in the sixth century—continue the story of Joseph of Arimathea after the Crucifixion.

It is said that Joseph was helped to take down the body of Jesus from the Cross by his son, Josephes, on whose shirt dripped some blood and sweat. Joseph immediately got two small vials or cruets in which he managed to collect a few drops and thus preserved the first and holiest of relics. After the burial, he was interrogated by the Sanhedrin and, for reaffirming his belief in Christ, was imprisoned, but was released by the Risen Lord and told to remain for forty days in his own house at Arimathea. He joined the other disciples in time to see the last of the Resurrection appearances and to witness the Ascension.

When, after Pentecost, the Apostles went, as they were bidden, to preach the Gospel to all nations, John, the Beloved Disciple to whom Jesus had entrusted the care of His mother, was sent to Ephesus and Joseph of Arimathea remained with his niece until her earthly life was ended. He then made his way, with his son Josephes, to St. Philip to whom had been given the task of evangelizing Gaul. In the year 63, while Peter and Paul were still in Rome, Philip decided that the Gospel must be taken to Britain. He appointed twelve missionaries for this task and at their head put Joseph who, because of his previous knowledge of Britain, was deemed the most obviously suitable person. The little company, of whom Josephes was one, set sail, rounded the Cornish coast, and landed in Wales. Here they were met with some hostility—probably on account of the strength of Druidism in these parts —and made their way eastward until they came to the territory of King Aviragus. Though he refused to be baptized, he listened to them courte-

"The little company . . . rounded the Cornish coast . . ."

ously and—so writes the Norman historian, William of Malmesbury, in 1135, basing his account on an earlier text—"because they came from far and merely required a modest competence for their life, at their request granted them a certain island, surrounded by woods, thickets and marshes, called by its inhabitants Ynys-witrin, on the confines of the kingdom."

Ynys-witrin: the Glassy Isle: Glastonbury.

In those days, the sea, now fourteen miles away, lapped the foot of the Tor, the five-hundred-foot high conical hill which dominates the landscape. The two smaller hills, Weary-all Hill and Chalice Hill, the Tor's attendant satellites, now standing among meadows and orchards, were surrounded by marshland. The river Brue, running through the valley, added its waters to the isolating elements.

Three centuries before the coming of the first Christians, the local Celtic inhabitants had made it a secret place of safety—a lake-village of the same type as those found in Switzerland. The water was their moat, giving security to their round, wattle huts beneath the Tor where they lived in self-contained community. From archaeological finds, we know that they were influenced by the Mediterranean culture, for the lovely designs on their pottery are undoubtedly inspired by it. Though they were in so remote a spot, there were communications by land and water with the civilization in the tin-trade area, then at the peak of its prosperity, and it may be that they had deliberately chosen, as others were later to choose, to retire to Glastonbury as a haven of refuge and peace from the savage exigencies of the world! In the end, however, they did not escape it. Not long before the Christian era, a wave of more efficient and warlike Celtic invaders, the Belgae, eventually reached and destroyed the Lake Village.

The name of Ynys-witrin, the Isle of Glass, has never been satisfactorily explained. Some think it referred to the blue-green color of the water; others, to a plant used for making woad. Nor is there any certainty about its age, except that it is older than the Anglo-Saxon name, Glaestingaburg. But the place had another name, which was to become famous in romantic legend. The Isle of Glass was also Avalon of the apple-trees and the Tor was the great hill towering over the Isle of the Dead, to the summit of which spirits were summoned for their departure for the Celtic Paradise.

There is a very early tradition about this embodied in the life of one of the saintly Christian hermits who came to Glastonbury in Saxon times. "The tale," as an authority has put it, "clearly embodies a folk-belief in no way derived from literary sources."

The saint, Collen, in his cell on the lower slopes of the Tor received a message bidding him go to the top of the hill to meet Gwyn, King of the Fairies and leader of the Wild Hunt.* After two refusals, he decided to answer the summons and, armed with holy water, arrived at the peak. Here, floating magically in the air above the summit, he saw a mansion in which were youths and maidens, retainers and musicians. In the midst of it sat King Gwyn on a chair of gold. "Have you ever seen men better dressed than these, in their liveries of red and blue?" asked Gwyn, after greeting Collen affably. "Their dress is good," replied the hermit, "but the red is the red of burning fire and the blue is the blue of cold." And as he threw the holy water in all directions, the mansion and its occupants suddenly vanished and he was left alone on the Tor with nothing but grass stirring in the wind.

The story is, of its kind, a conventional one which has many parallels in various countries; but it is significant that in the mythology of the Druids the mansion is a palace of glass, receiving in its transparent walls the souls of the blessed. This, surely, considering the actual circumstances and beliefs of the time, is the explanation of Glas-

* This Hunt, in which the souls of the dead are separated from their bodies is, in one form or another, a feature of all European folk-lore.

tonbury-Avalon's name, The Isle of Glass.* That the succeeding centuries tried to exorcise "the ancient gods pursuing" we know because a chapel was built on the top of the Tor and dedicated to St. Michael the Archangel, the conqueror of the Dark Powers. The ruins of its larger successor are still there, crowning the Tor; and the visitor to-day who looks at it with knowledgeable eyes may understand something of the atmosphere which greeted Joseph of Arimathea when he arrived at this hidden Celtic island, firm in its Druidic beliefs, and, in despair, planted his staff on Weary-all Hill with a prayer to another God.

* As far as I know, this theory has never before been suggested.

4

JOSEPH AND HIS eleven anchorites made their cells near a well at the foot of the Tor. To-day the well is known as Chalice Well and the house in whose grounds it now stands as the Anchor Inn. It is a two-chambered Druidical well of immense antiquity. Architects aver that the stone bears marks of being cut by flint instruments. The spring yields about 25,000 gallons a day and never lessens. About the middle of the eighteenth century, its water was, for a short time, in great demand as a cure for asthma, phthsis and cancer. In the twentieth century it saved the town of Glastonbury from the droughts of 1921 and 1922. The well bridges the centuries and identifies the spot where the Twelve lived so acceptably that the successors of King Aviragus "although pagans, observing their pious mode of life, presented to each of them a portion of land and, at their request, confirmed the twelve portions to them after the heathen manner: and it is believed that the Twelve Hides get their name from them to this day." Thus William of Malmesbury.

However the Twelve Hides came into being, they continued in history. The exact measure of a hide is uncertain. It was a portion of land, variable in extent but sufficient to support one family and capable of being cultivated in a year by one ox-drawn plow. Eight hides constituted a "knight's fee." An average hide was about a hundred and twenty acres.

In the Domesday Book they are entered thus: "This Glastonbury Church possesses in its own Villa twelve hides of land which have never paid tax." Ultimately the Twelve Hides became the name of the district round the Tor, several miles in extent, over which the Abbot of Glastonbury had supreme jurisdiction, including the power of life and death.

The great event of Joseph's sojourn at Glastonbury was the building of the church—the first Christian church to be built in Britain. Some say the commission to erect it was given to Joseph by Christ Himself; others that he was commanded to do so by the Archangel Gabriel, who had once announced to Mary that she was to be the mother of the Lord. The church was to be dedicated to her. So the hermits started to build what was to be known as the Wattle Church, made of mud and reeds and "twisted twigs," sixty feet long and twenty-six feet wide, the dimensions of the Tabernacle. Here Joseph set up an image of the Virgin Mary, carved by himself. Here, in due time, he was buried, with the two cruets beside him. That little space was, indeed, "the holiest earth in England."

Four hundred years later—that is to say, a century before the "reconversion" of England by St. Augustine—a British bard, Melkin (or Maelgwn) described how, in "Avalon's Island," Joseph of Arimathea

Hath found perpetual sleep:
And he lies on a two-forked line
Next the south corner of an oratory
Fashioned of wattles
For the adoring of a mighty Virgin.
For Joseph had with him
In his sarcophagus,
Two cruets white and silver,
Filled with blood and sweat
Of the Prophet Jesus.
When his sarcophagus
Shall be found entire, intact,
In time to come, it shall be seen
And shall be open unto all the world.

Thenceforth nor water nor the dew of heaven
Shall fail the dwellers of that ancient isle.

In the medieval life of Joseph, the little church
is referred to thus:

So Joseph dyd as the aungell hym bad
And wrought there an ymage of our lady;
For to serve hyr great devotion he had
And that same ymage is still at Glastonbury
In the same church: there ye may it see
For it was the first, as I understande,
That ever was sene in this countre;
For Joseph it made wyth his owne hande.

And coming nearer to our own day, Tennyson
has epitomized the tradition in *Idylls of the King:*

From our old books I know
That Joseph came of old to Glastonbury,
And there the heathen Prince, Arviragus,
Gave him an isle of marsh whereon to build;
And there he built with wattles from the marsh
A little lonely church in days of yore.

The inscription on Joseph's grave was said to
be: "Ad Britannos veni post Christum sepelivi.
Docui. Quievi." "I came to the Britons after I
buried Christ. I taught. I rest."

When in the year 597, Augustine arrived from
Rome to convert the Anglo-Saxons to Christianity, Glastonbury was still a Christian center with

". . . the hermits started to build . . . the Wattle
Church, made of mud and reeds and 'twisted
twigs' . . ."

an unbroken tradition. The invaders had not penetrated so far west. So when Augustine's helper Paulinus visited the Isle of Glass which, in the meantime, had become an Isle of Saints, he found the Wattle Church still there. To protect it from the weather, he built round it a superstructure of wooden planks and pieces of lead. There it remained until, at the beginning of the eighth century, the great Wessex monarch, King Ina (a direct ancestor of Queen Elizabeth II) decided to devote himself to the rebuilding of Glastonbury. As a place of unalterable holiness, he left the encased Wattle Church alone and built the new abbey closer to the hill-side. It was finished in the year 704 and the charter was signed in the "Lignea Basilica" itself: "In order that the Church of Our Lord Jesus Christ and the eternal Virgin Mary, as it is first in the kingdom of Britain and the source and fountain of all religion, may obtain surpassing dignity and privilege. . . . I appoint and establish that all lands, places and possessions of St. Mary of Glastonbury be free from all royal taxes and works."

The end of the Wattle Church came on May 25, 1184, when the Abbey was burnt in a disastrous fire. From the flames, one thing only was saved—the antique image of Our Lady of Glastonbury which Joseph of Arimathea had made more than a thousand years before.

5

WHETHER OR NOT you believe the story of Joseph of Arimathea depends, in the last analysis, on your view of history. If your subconscious belief—sub-conscious, because a moment's thought will dispel the foolishness—is that everything that has happened has been recorded and that all the records are true, then you will reject it as a legend for which there is no documentary proof. But if you approach history as a living story of the past, involving men and motives and actions not so different from today's, you will give tradition its true weight and tend to accept it if it does not conflict with probabilities. In history, more than in any other study, the relevant counsel is: "The man who thinks himself wise believes nothing until it is proved, but the man who is wise believes everything until it is disproved."

In the case of Glastonbury, the inescapable question is: "Why Joseph of Arimathea?" If the story is nothing but a late invention to glorify the British church, why not postulate one of the Apostles? Why should not St. Philip himself have crossed the Channel or St. Andrew have included Britain in a missionary journey or St. James have come over from Spain? It is arguable that St. Paul himself, following the tin-trade route from Spain, visited these shores. He, had it been merely a legendary matter, would have been a more impressive founder than the Arimathean.*

May not the reason of the powerful and persisting tradition about Joseph be, quite simply, because it happened to be true? We know, with certainty, that, by an ancient and well-organized trade-route, any Eastern business man could have come to Britain as naturally as today an executive can fly from New York to London. If Joseph was, as one tradition asserts, "in the tin-trade" and, according to another, the uncle of the Virgin Mary, there would be nothing strange in his bringing Jesus with him on some journey during the

* Clement of Rome, writing in 100 A.D., mentions Paul as "arriving at the extremity of the West" (which is usually taken as meaning Spain). Theodoret, a scholar and commentator, writing three centuries later, says that, from Spain, Paul passed on to "the islands that are situated in the sea."

eighteen years about which we have no recorded information on the life of Christ. Had he this first-hand knowledge of the country, he was the likeliest person to be appointed to evangelize it in later years. From this, the rest proceeds. At no point does the story conflict with probability; and if it cannot be "proved" neither can it be disproved.

And the flowering Hawthorn? The most sceptical must grant, on botanical evidence, that it came from the East and that it existed—until in more modern times shoots were taken from it—at Glastonbury alone. If it could have been brought back by a pilgrim or a Crusader, why could it not have been brought by Joseph? The theory which gives it the later origin seems to have no reason behind it but an attempt to discredit the former. Either is equally possible.

The story of its first flowering involves, indeed, a miraculous element, which by its analogy to other such tales—as, for example, the Pope's staff in the tale of Tannhauser—suggests pious embroidery. But no one who accepts the original miracle of God becoming Man in Palestine, can refuse to accept the possibility of other miracles. He can only, as he is bidden to do by the Church, try to assess their authenticity by reference to the ordinary canons of evidence and probability which he would apply to any other occurrence. But whether one accepts or not the immediate and miraculous flowering, there is nothing impossible in the idea of the staff being planted in the ground and eventually blossoming. And the date of the phenomenon would be Christmas Day.

And here again one is met by a curious fact which is often overlooked. December 25 was not celebrated as Christmas Day until well into the fourth century. Till then the date was—as in the Eastern Church it still is—January 6, which is now the Feast of the Epiphany. And it is on that date, at the end of the "Twelve Days of Christmas," as we have it, that the Hawthorn flowered.

Whatever may be thought of the authenticity of Joseph of Arimathea as the founder of Christian Glastonbury, his successors, including the patron saints of Ireland and of Wales as well as the first British historian, stride certainly into history. An early writer, referring to the reputed tombs of the first hermits, says: "We know not whether they really repose here, although we have read that they sojourned in this place for nine years but here dwelt assuredly many of their disciples, ever twelve in number, who in imitation of them led a hermit's life until unto them came St. Patrick, the great Apostle of the Irish and first abbot of the hallowed spot. Here, too, rests St. Benen, the disciple of St. Patrick; here St. Gildas, the historian of the British; here St. David, bishop of Menevia and here the holy hermit In-dractus with his seven companions, all sprung from the royal race. Here rest the relics of a band of holy Irish pilgrims who, returning from a visit to the shrines of Rome, turned aside to Glaston-bury out of love to St. Patrick's memory and were martyred in a village named Shapwick. Hither, not long after, their remains were brought by Ina, our glorious king."

Patrick, who has come to be thought of as something exclusively Irish, was the most cos-mopolitan of saints. Born of aristocratic Roman parents when Britain was still a province of Rome, he was kidnapped as a young man and carried into slavery in Ireland. Escaping, he made his way to Gaul where he was trained by the great St. Ger-main and chosen to accompany him to Britain for his controversy with Pelagius at St. Albans. Subsequently Patrick went to Rome and was charged by the Pope with the conversion of Ire-land. After he had accomplished this task, accord-ing to the Glastonbury story, he crossed to Somer-set and—as he is reported as saying in a late document which, nevertheless, is based on an earlier tradition—"by the guidance of God, who is the life and the way, I chanced upon the isle of Ynis-witrin, wherein I found a place holy and ancient, chosen and sanctified by God in honor of Mary the pure Virgin, the Mother of God: and there I found certain brethren imbued with the rudiments of the Catholic faith and of pious conversation. . . . And since we were all of one heart and one mind, we chose to dwell together, and eat and drink in common, and sleep in the same house." Patrick is said to have ruled the little community for nine years and, when he died in 472, to have been buried in the Wattle Church on the right of the altar.

David, born a quarter of a century after Patrick's death, was believed to have come to Glastonbury to dedicate a church to the Virgin Mary, but, being shown by Christ in a vision that the Old Church was so dedicated, built another near it. After many travels he returned to the Glastonbury community of monks to die and was buried near St. Patrick.

Thus, by the middle of the sixth century—more than thirty years before the coming of St. Augustine and the mission from Rome—Glastonbury was pre-eminent as a Christian center. She linked the British, the Irish and the Welsh strains and carried them back in continuity to apostolic times. She had taken over the mystery and mysticism of pre-Christian Celtic beliefs which had gathered round the Isle of Glass and had given them a different shape and meaning in the light of a new Revelation. So, from the very beginning, there was seen her power of reconciliation and her pride of continuity which was to make the soon-to-be-established Canterbury appear a little parochial and to justify her own status as "the second Rome." And now it was as Avalon that she awaited the coming of Arthur.

6

THE DAY IS fortunately over when one needed to discuss, even for dismissal, the Victorian theory that the story of Arthur is a Sun-God myth. The fact that the King was to become legendary in literature, even sometimes to the point of absurdity, in no way imperils his historicity, even if, in that dark age, it is difficult to see him clearly.

The Roman legions withdrew from Britain in 410, leaving the land to be gradually infiltrated and conquered by the Saxon invaders. The British, in 446, unable to defend themselves, addressed to the great Roman general who was engaged against the Huns on the continent the despairing cry: "To Aëtius, three times consul, the groans of the Britons: The barbarians drive us to the sea, the sea drives us to the barbarians; between these two kinds of death we are either massacred or drowned." But Aëtius could not help them. He had a more important and more difficult battle to fight. A Romano-British leader, however, living in the yet unconquered villa-civilization of the west (probably Gloucestershire) did arise. Gildas the historian, the Glastonbury monk, writing in the 540's, refers to him by name. After mentioning the Britons who fled to Brittany to escape the Saxons, he says: "Others remained in their country albeit with fear, and trusted their lives to hills and precipitous mountains, dense forests and crags by the sea. When some time had passed and the most cruel of the plunderers had returned home, this remnant was strengthened by God. To them, from all sides, our wretched citizens flocked as eagerly as bees when a storm is brewing . . . Their leader was Ambrosius Aurelianus." Nennius, the next historian after Gildas, refers to him as the Supreme King of the Britons, which is generally supposed to have been his revival of the Roman title, *Comes Britanniarum,* the Count of the Britons, by which he imposed unity on his command and consolidated the British resistance. For forty years the war dragged on, from Ambrosius's first attack on Hengist in Kent in the early 470's to the shattering victory of Mount Badon (the modern Bath in Somerset) in

517, which gave some peace to the land. It had been predominantly a defensive action, interspersed by guerilla raids, and the British had ultimately withdrawn into their held territory in the West—Wiltshire and Somerset,—which they had protected by a fifty-mile earthwork known as the Wansdyke. It remains today as a mute memorial of the Ambrosian resistance.

In the later phases of the war, the leader of the British was Artorius, who was born about 470 and, on reaching manhood, became Ambrosius Aurelianus's chief lieutenant, on whom he eventually bestowed the title of *Comes Britanniarum.* Arthur had Roman blood and formed his own company of picked horsemen which he trained in the arts of war on the Roman pattern. Wherever he appeared, his cavalry constituted the superior force which won the day. He was, even when Ambrosius was in titular command, the unquestioned *dux bellorum,* leader in the battles. Nennius gives this account of him: "Arthur fought against the Saxons alongside the Kings of the Britons, but he himself was the leader in the battles. The first battle was at the mouth of the river which is called Glein. The next four were on the banks of another river, which is called Dubglas. The sixth was upon the river which is called Bassas. The seventh was in the wood of Celidon. The eighth was by Castle Guinnion, in which Arthur carried on his shoulders an image of St. Mary Ever-Virgin, and on that day the pagans were put to flight, and there was a great slaughter of them, through the strength of Our Lord Jesus Christ and of the holy Mary his maiden-mother. The ninth was in the City of the Legion. The tenth was on the bank of the river which is called Tribruit.* The eleventh was on the hill called Agned. The twelfth was on Mount Badon, in which—on that one day—there fell in one onslaught of Arthur's, nine hundred and sixty men."

After the victory of Mount Badon (which is, by general consent, Badbury Rings in Dorset) the country had peace for twenty years until, as the *Annales Cambriae* record, in 538 was "the battle of Camlaun in which Arthur and Medraut (Modred) were slain; and there was death in England." In that golden interim, Arthur reigned at his court at Camelot—which is Cadbury Castle, overlooking the Vale of Avalon.

Of his connection with Glastonbury, many stories are told. Giraldus Cambrensis, whose twelfth century history was based on older records, says that King Arthur had great devotion to Our Lady of Glastonbury and that he enriched her shrine with many costly presents. He had her

* It is perhaps worthy of remark that this battle is commemorated in an early Welsh poem in which Bedwyr (Sir Bedivere) is mentioned as one of the warriors.

image painted on his shield and it is tempting to think that it was this very image that he carried on his shoulders in the battle near Castle Guinnion.

The last fatal battle of Camlan which Arthur fought against his base-born son, Modred, is famous in the literature of the Arthurian cycle, but it may be worth quoting here the early prose account written by Matthew of Westminster, a Benedictine monk of the Middle Ages. "After a great part of the day had passed, at last Arthur rushed on, borne onward by a lion's spirit, against that part of the army in which he knew that Modred was: and making himself a way with his sword and scattering the enemy, he made a most bloody slaughter of them, scattered their close ranks and drove them different ways. The battle grew thick and fierce and the air rattled with the clang of the blows. Therefore Modred fell and with him many thousands of soldiers and so, by favour of God, the victory fell to Arthur. But alas! he was mortally wounded and was carried from thence to the island of Avalon, which is now called Glastonia, to be healed of his wounds . . . The dying king kept himself from sight, so that his enemies might not insult his misfortunes and his friends be grieved, on which account, as the historians say nothing of the death of Arthur or of his burial, the nation of the Britons, out of the greatness of their affection for him, contend that he is still alive."

As the battle was presumably fought by the river Cam, near Arthur's capital at Cadbury Castle, Avalon was, from every point of view, the place to which the wounded King would wish to be taken. And there, five and a half centuries later, the tomb was found. Even today, the bridge over the river Brue, a mile from Glastonbury, is known as Pontperles (Pons periculus) because it was the place where Sir Bedivere, at Arthur's bidding, threw the famous sword, Excalibur.

It was after the destruction by fire of the Abbey in 1184 that King Henry II, on one of his journeys in Wales, was told by a bard that Arthur's grave was identifiable. The King himself was profoundly affected by the fate of the Abbey, which by that time had become a landmark and a glory of all Christendom, and he took upon himself the restoration of it. "Because whatsoever a man soweth that shall he also reap," he proclaimed, "I, in the act of laying the foundation of Glastonbury (which, being in my hands, has been reduced to aches by fire) do decree . . . that, God willing, it shall be magnificently completed by myself or by my heirs." The grave of Arthur, according to the information at his disposal, lay between two pyramids in the Abbey. The Abbot, on his instructions, located the area, roped it off and started

". . . it was the place where Sir Bedivere, at Arthur's
bidding, threw the famous sword, Excalibur."

to dig. After considerable labor, seven feet below ground, they came on a leaden cross which, on one side, bore the inscription: *"Hic jacet sepultus inclytus Rex Arturus in Insula Avallonia"*—"Here lies buried the renowned King Arthur in the Isle of Avalon." * They continued to dig feverishly, the monks helping the laborers. After another nine feet—sixteen feet below ground level—they unearthed a hollowed-out tree trunk, the coffin of an enormous skeleton.

The bones belonged to no ordinary man. His shin bone was measured against that of the tallest monk present and exceeded it by three fingers' breadth. The skull showed the marks of ten or more wounds. One, the death-blow, had smashed it in by the left ear and it had not rehealed. At the foot of the huge coffin was another, smaller one. There were strands of hair, plaited, on this skeleton. A monk touched them and they crumbled in the air. The golden hair of Guinevere had fallen to dust.

Giraldus Cambrensis—Gerald of Wales—may have been present at the exhumation. Certainly he went to the Abbey immediately afterwards to

* This cross may still be in existence in some forgotten family attic in England. It was seen at the Abbey just before the Dissolution and Camden, in 1607, drew a picture of it. In the eighteenth century it was the property of a Mr. Chancellor Hughes of Wells. Since then all trace has been lost. It is, surely, one of the most worthy objects of antiquarian research.

satisfy himself about the matter. He spoke to the monk whose shinbone was shorter than Arthur's. He examined the other finds and, in his history published four years later, he narrated the circumstance.

From the point of view of today one piece of evidence is conclusive. The method of burial in a hollowed-out tree trunk was that used by the Celtic Britons, but it was unknown to the Middle Ages. Had the men of 1190 wished to perpetrate a prestige-bringing fraud, they would undoubtedly have used a stone sarcophagus. "The description which they actually gave is so odd from their point of view, yet so plausible from ours, that one may well feel bound to believe it—substantially." So writes Mr. Geoffrey Ashe, the modern authority on Glastonbury, who errs always, wisely enough, on the side of caution. And though, obviously, it is impossible to "prove" that the skeleton was Arthur's, it would seem foolish to reject the hypothesis when every circumstance points to its acceptance. No one doubted it at the time and when, in 1191, Henry II's son, King Richard the Lion Hearted went south on his Crusade, he gave to Tancred of Sicily, as a gift of the highest honor, the very sword that had once been named Excalibur.

Another crusading monarch, King Edward I and his Queen, kept Easter at Glastonbury in

1278 and wished to see for themselves the relics of Arthur, who had by that time been reinterred in the great church of the restored Abbey. They carried the relics in solemn procession to the high altar, Edward bearing the bones of Arthur and his Queen those of Guinevere. Wrapped in the most costly cloths, they were deposited in a new and splendid tomb near the High Altar, which was sealed with the King's signet.* So Arthur came to his last resting-place.

* Today a notice marks the place. The tomb, like the rest of the Abbey, was despoiled and destroyed during the Reformation.

7

AS GLASTONBURY had been the center of the Romano-British stand against the invading Saxons, so, in the ninth century, it was to be the center of the crucial resistance of the now Christianized Saxons against the new wave of pagan invaders, the Danes. In Arthur's place stood the only king to whom has been, in British history, accorded the title of "the Great"—Alfred of Wessex. In 878 the Danes had reached Glastonbury, fired and looted the churches and then withdrawn. A few miles to the southwest of Glastonbury was another island in the marshes named Athelney. Here, a fugitive in hiding, Alfred was in despair, with only a few of his followers left to him.

Alfred knew Glastonbury well. His half-brother Neot had been sacristan there and the King himself had great devotion to Our Lady of Glastonbury. At this nadir of his fortunes, he traveled the nine miles from Athelney to the Abbey to make special intercession at her shrine. He then returned to muster what men he could and, certain of victory in spite of the Danes' immense superiority of fighting men, gave chase to them and overtook them at Ethandune—the modern Edington, in Wiltshire, near the end of the escarpment of the North Downs, at a place which is now marked with a White Horse. On the night before the battle, Alfred had a dream in which Neot appeared to him, in splendid apparel and promised victory. As Arthur had borne the image of Our Lady all day in one of his battles, so Alfred now trusted in her promise to defend the Christian against the pagans. Readers of G. K. Chesterton's magnificent *Ballad of the White Horse* will remember how, when all seemed lost,

> The King looked up and what he saw
> Was a great light like death,
> For Our Lady stood on the standards rent,
> As lonely and as innocent
> As when between white walls she went
> And the lilies of Nazareth.
> One instant in a still light
> He saw Our Lady then,

Her dress was soft as western sky,
And she was a queen most womanly—
But she was a queen of men.
Over the iron forest
He saw Our Lady stand,
Her eyes were sad withouten art,
And seven swords were in her heart—
But one was in her hand.

and how, at the last despairing rally of the Christians, Alfred saw the miracle and cried:

"The Mother of God goes over them,
On dreadful cherubs borne;
And the psalm is roaring above the rune
And the Cross goes over the sun and moon,
Endeth the battle of Ethandune
With the blowing of a horn."

In the political history of England, the warfare is merely a strife of Danes and Saxons from which the Saxons under Alfred emerged, surprisingly, victorious; but in the history of Christendom it is as much a landmark in the Christian-pagan struggle as the battle of Chalons when Aëtius turned back the Huns under Attila at Chalons or Roland's engagement with the Saracens at Roncesvalles. And this is the truer perspective, which becomes more apparent when Glastonbury is given its proper place in the story of Alfred. Guthrum the Dane was baptized, with thirty of his chiefs, and concluded the treaty of peace with Alfred at Wedmore, six miles to the northwest of Glastonbury.

Alfred died in 901. About 909 was born Dunstan, perhaps the only other man in the pre-Conquest period who approaches Arthur and Alfred in greatness, at Baltonsborough, five miles from Glastonbury. He went to school at the Abbey, where his uncle, Athelm, now Bishop of Bath and Wells had been a pupil before him. One night Dunstan dreamt that a majestic old man, dressed in white, took him round the Abbey, enriched with new chapels and other buildings, and told him that one day he would be the Abbot.

The dream came true. After a short time at court, he was ordained at the age of 27 by his kinsman, St. Alphege, then Bishop of Winchester. He spent some time at Court but intrigues and jealousies sowed dissension between him and the young King Edmund, who dismissed him. The court was at Cheddar, at the foot of the great rocky gorge through the Mendip hills, when Dunstan prepared to take his leave of it. He did not accompany the King on a hunt in Mendip Forest, but stayed to confer with some visiting ambassadors, intending to travel with them out of the country. Meanwhile Edmund's horse was rushing to the very edge of the precipice in pursuit of a stag and the rider was powerless to control it. With death in sight, the King prayed and vowed that, were his life spared, he would make amends to Dunstan. The horse swerved and saved itself and its rider and Edmund made his way by the gentler path to Cheddar. At once he implemented his promise. He took Dunstan with him to Glastonbury, twelve miles distant. Together they prayed before the altar. Then Edmund gave Dunstan the kiss of peace, took him by the hand and seated him on the Abbot's throne, promising him all the help he needed. This was in 943. Three years later the king was murdered by an outlaw and Dunstan buried him in the Abbey.

For the next ten years or so, Dunstan's main care was Glastonbury. He himself lived in holy simplicity in a tiny cell whose foundations may still be seen not far from where the Wattle Church stood. But he made the Abbey into a great Benedictine foundation, using the money which the Crown allowed him, to remodel King Ina's church. William of Malmesbury described it thus: "The result of Dunstan's labours was that as far as the design of the ancient structure allowed, a basilica was produced of great extent in both directions; wherein if aught be lacking in seemliness and beauty, there is, at any rate, no want of necessary room."

In addition to the church itself, he built adequate living-quarters for the monks; he remodeled the burying-places, collecting all the bones of his predecessors in the abbacy into one coffin (which was not discovered until 1928); he organized a land-reclamation scheme of the marshy ground which was transformed into grazing meadows and arable fields; he started the manufacture of special glassware; and, above all, he transcribed and illuminated valuable manuscripts and composed music which he himself played on the harp.

Eventually Dunstan, who died in 988, became Archbishop of Canterbury and the chief adviser of the Crown, but his greatest monument was Glastonbury. He was buried in Canterbury Cathedral, but the Glastonbury monks insisted that, after the attack of the Danes on Canterbury in 1012, his relics were saved (or, as the Canterburians would express it, stolen) and reinterred at Glastonbury. The dispute between the two great foundations on this score lasted until the destruction of Glastonbury at the Reformation.

The Glastonbury story, as narrated by William of Malmesbury, was: "Two who had charge of the matter take a wooden coffin, suitably prepared for the purpose and paint it on the inside, and on the right side they put the S. and on the left the D, intending that they should stand for the name of Sanctus Dunstanus. Putting the relics into this coffin, they bury it, beneath a stone, taken out

". . . he transcribed and illuminated valuable manuscripts and composed music which he himself played
on the harp . . ."

for the purpose, in the 'Larger Church', by the side of the holy water stoup, on the right hand side of the entrance of the monks; everybody else was ignorant of the place altogether. There for a hundred and seventy years it lay * the secret being committed to one at a time, according to the arranged plan. But a young monk is said to have prevailed upon his master to hint engimatically at the place of burial and the secret became known and all was found as has been described."

The Canterbury side of the matter was to deny the story *in toto* and to insist that the remains of Dunstan were intact in his tomb there. It was not until 1508 that the then Archbishop of Canterbury, to settle the matter, opened the shrine and reported that it contained all the principal bones of St. Dunstan. Needless to say, Glastonbury contested the Archbishop's accuracy and the truth of it is never likely to be known. What is certain is that Glastonbury itself, in its new and more splendid form, was Dunstan's monument. And here, less than fifty years after Dunstan's death, occurred one more of the great reconciling moments which are the recurring marks of the place's history.

In the third Danish war, Edmund Ironside and Canute fought each other. The Ironside, by his

* that is to say, till just before the great fire of 1184.

own request, was buried by the high altar of Glastonbury. To the tomb went Canute—a devout Christian—to pray and to drape it with a magnificent pall, embroidered by skilled Saxon hands with multi-colored peacocks.

8

BEFORE PROCEEDING with the story of Glastonbury, we may look at it through the eyes of William of Malmesbury, who saw the Old Church before the fire swept it away: "This church is certainly the oldest I am acquainted with in England and from this circumstance derives its name. In it are preserved the mortal remains of many saints, nor is any corner of the church destitute of the ashes of the holy. The very floor, inlaid with polished stones, and the sides of the altar, and even the altar itself above and beneath, are laden with the multitude of relics. Moreover, in the pavement may be remarked on every side stones designedly interlaid in triangles and squares and sealed with lead, under which if I believe some sacred mystery to be contained, I do no injustice to religion. The antiquity and the multitude of its saints have endued the place with so much sanctity that at night scarcely anyone presumes to keep vigil there. He who is conscious of pollution shudders throughout his whole frame; no one ever brought hawk or horses within the confines of the neighbouring cemetery who did not depart injured, either in them or in himself. Those persons who, about to undergo the ordeal of fire or water, did there put up their petitions, have in every instance that can now be recollected, except one, exulted in their escape. If any person erected a building in its vicinity, which by its shade obstructed the light of the church, it forthwith became a ruin. And it is sufficiently evident that the men of that province had no oath more frequent or more sacred than to swear by the Old Church, and from fear of swift vengeance avoided nothing so much as perjury in this respect . . .

"There are numbers of documents which prove how extremely venerable this place was held to be by the chief persons of the country, who there more especially chose to await the day of resurrection under the protection of the Mother of God."

William of Malmesbury's book, written in 1125, was dedicated to Henry de Blois, who, as Abbot of Glastonbury, was to raise the Abbey's fame to even greater heights. Henry de Blois, a grandson of William the Conqueror, had been trained for an ecclesiastical career at the Benedictine monastery of Cluny. He was only thirty when his uncle, Henry I called him to take office at Glastonbury. Here he built nobly—"the bell-tower, the chapter-house, cloister, lavatory, refectory and dormitory; also the infirmary with its chapel; a spacious gate-way, remarkable for its squared stones; a large brew-house and stables for many horses; and besides these works he gave many princely ornaments to the church." *

The finest "ornament," however, Henry de Blois had the good fortune to find. It was known as the Great Sapphire and was a magnificent array of precious stones set in gold and silver and intended to be hung over the altar. Legend had it that it had been brought to Glastonbury by St. David after his visit to Jerusalem. When the Danish peril was at its height, the monks had hidden it and now Henry de Blois discovered it in a secret cupboard behind the door of the Old Church.

The royal Abbot did, however, spend much of his own fortune on the Abbey—tapestries, altar

* So wrote Adam de Domerham, who in the thirteenth century was sacristan at Glastonbury and who continued William of Malmesbury's chronicle.

furniture, books and vestments. When he was appointed Bishop of Winchester, he asked the Pope's permission to remain Abbot of Glastonbury, which he may indeed have regarded as the greater title. When his weak and amiable brother, Stephen, became King of England and provoked the savage civil war in which, men said, "God and His saints slept," Henry, appointed Papal Legate, became even more powerful and made no secret of his disapprobation of some of his brother's policies, and even at one point sided with his rival for the throne. The Abbot of Glastonbury became the real Lord of England; and in the political and civil chaos he raised the prestige of the church in general and his Abbey of Glastonbury in particular to a new eminence. Glastonbury indeed became *Roma secunda,* the second Rome.

Henry of Blois died thirteen years before the great fire destroyed the Abbey and another rebuilding began. On the site of the Wattle Church, encased in its boards, rose the Church of St. Mary, whose ruins we can see today and admire in them the exquisitely molded arches and doorways, the interlaced arcading and the chiseled bosses which make it, even in ruin, "a jewel of Romanesque architecture."

To the excavation of Arthur's tomb, reference has already been made; and it seems that with the destruction of the physical link with Joseph of

Arimathea, though his church went up in flames, his influence returned in another way, connecting him with Arthur in a sense which has lasted through the centuries.

Forty years after the fire there appeared a book which, in its epilogue, claims: "The Latin from whence this history was drawn into Romance was taken in the Isle of Avalon, in a holy house of religion that standeth at the head of the Moors Adventurous, there where King Arthur and Queen Guinevere lie, according to the witness of the good men religious that are therein, that have the whole history thereof."

The book is *Perlesvaus,* which we call *The High History of the Holy Grail.*

9

THE HOLY GRAIL, which was to become identified in its Christian form with the Chalice
which was used at the Last Supper, originated in
paganism as a miraculous dish or bowl or cauldron which satisfies all needs. In Celtic folklore it
was the cauldron of Annwn (Hades) and was connected with that Gwyn, King of the Fairies and
Leader of the Wild Hunt, who was supposed to live
at the top of Glastonbury Tor. In early Welsh
bardic literature, not yet Christianized, Arthur
and his knights go in quest of the cauldron, or grail.

At what point Christian romancers appropriated
the Grail and made it "Holy" it is difficult to deter-
mine, but it was sometime in the late twelfth
century. The great debate of Christendom at that

time was on the manner in which the Lord's Body and Blood was present in the Eucharist—the matter being settled at the Lateran Council of 1215 by the definition of transubstantiation. It was therefore natural enough that in the preceding years, the romances should deal in their own way with the intellectual question which was agitating Europe. It was about 1190, it will be remembered, that Arthur's grave was opened at Glastonbury. And it was at the same date that the first Christian Grail romance (or, at least, the first to which reference is still possible) was written by Robert de Borron. In it, he identified the Grail with the Chalice and asserted that it had been brought to Glastonbury by Joseph of Arimathea.

In a sense it was comprehensible enough a merging, though up to this point there had been no suggestion that Joseph brought with him anything but the two cruets, which are still his emblems in ecclesiastical art. Accrediting him with the Chalice is a late invention, answering to the needs of a theological romance, which did not take rise till more than a thousand years after his death. Because it became so powerful, because Chalice Hill at Glastonbury is a reminder of the spot where he is supposed to have buried it, the later legend tends to discredit, in some eyes, the earlier story. But, in reality, it tells the other way. It was because the real Joseph was so surely established at Glastonbury that the legendary Joseph took shape there. The real Wattle Church became the romantic "Chapel of the Grail" where "the Grail appeared at the sacring of the Mass, in five several manners that none ought to tell, for the secret things of the sacrament ought none to tell openly but he unto whom God hath given it. King Arthur beheld the changes, the last whereof was the change into a chalice."

It is impossible to follow here the ramifications and interpretations of the Grail story, which forms an important field of scholarship in its own right, but one aspect, in connection with Glastonbury, must be noted. The Christianized Grail is inseparable from the Virgin Mary. As one of the Welsh poets writing at the time of the romances put it: "Christ, Son of Mary, my cauldron of pure descent." And Mr. Geoffrey Ashe, who has written on this particular matter with more perspicacity than any one else, has suggested that the true answer to the crucial question that must be asked if the Waste Land is to revivify: "Whom does the Grail serve?" is "Mary." Now, the one thing that Glastonbury was more than anything else and beyond all dispute, was the shrine of devotion to the Virgin Mary. From the building of the Wattle Church it had been so. It was on Our Lady of Glastonbury that both Arthur and Alfred had called for succour and their victories had made her become regarded as something which may be called, without irreverence, the Christian talisman of England. It was the saving of her image from the fire—presumably the statue accredited to Joseph of Arimathea—that was the miraculous comfort of the monks. She formed another, and the most potent, link between the Grail and Glastonbury. More than the connection of the folklore Arthur with the cauldron of Annwn at Avalon; more than the reputed coming of Joseph of Arimathea to the Glass Island; more than the existence of an Abbey of European fame, the *cultus* of Our Lady, stretching back to the very beginning of the Christian era, connected the Grail with Glastonbury. And in the centuries to come, fostered in part by the Grail romances, the influence increased so that England itself was known quite simply as "Our Lady's Dowry."

The transformation of the story of Joseph of Arimathea by the romancers is complete. According to de Borron's *Joseph,* he obtains the Chalice of the Last Supper as a keepsake and is imprisoned by the Jews for forty-two years. He is sustained miraculously by the Grail after Christ has appeared to him in a vision and taught him the secret words of consecration which no one can utter unless he has learnt the secret of the Great Sacrament to which the Grail is the key. Eventually Joseph is released by the Emperor Vespasian and, with a company of Christians, he takes the Grail to another country. Here, guided by the Holy Spirit, he constructs a square table as a symbol of the table of the Last Supper, with a place for the Grail facing the chair corresponding to that in which Jesus sat. He and his companions occupy the other chairs and, to a greater or lesser degree depending on their own holiness, they feel the beneficent effects of the Grail.

De Borron did not finish his work and that part which was to deal with Joseph's adventures in Britain was never written. It would have been interesting to see how his symbolism extended to Glastonbury. One thing, at least, is odd about it. The "square table" is undoubtedly part of some esoteric doctrine connected with the Grail or with Joseph. Was de Borron using some already known tradition at which, seventy years earlier and quite independently, William of Malmesbury had hinted in his description of the Church as he saw it—"in the pavement may be remarked on every side stones designedly interlaid in triangles and squares and sealed with lead, under which if I believe some sacred mystery to be contained I do no injustice to religion?" Had the "sacred mystery" referred to here any connection with the words used regarding the Chalice in the consecration at Mass—"the mystery of faith?" *

As the legendary Joseph grew, so interest in the real Joseph increased. In 1345 a man named

* They are used of the Cup only, not of the Host. They are usually supposed to have been originally the private devotion of Pope Anicetus who put the Consecration Prayer in its final form about 160 A.D.

John Blome, who claimed a special revelation on the subject, obtained permission from King Edward III to search for it. The place of burial had been specified in Melkin's prophecy:

> He lies on a two-forked line
> Next the south corner of an oratory
> Fashioned of wattles.

The site, of course, had been carefully preserved in the rebuilding, but the exact meaning of the *linea bifurcata,* the two-forked line, was and remains obscure from the point of view of practical excavation. John Blome did not find the body.

The monks accepted their ignorance but continued to trust the tradition that the body was there. On this matter we have a first-hand piece of evidence from William Good who was born at Glastonbury in 1527, survived the Dissolution and in the reign of Elizabeth I went abroad and became a Jesuit. He wrote: "The monks never knew for certain the place of this saint's burying or pointed it out. They said the body was hidden most carefully, either there or on a hill near Montacute called Hamdon Hill * and that when his body should be found the whole world would wend their way thither on account of the miracles worked there.

* about fifteen miles due south of Glastonbury.

"Among other things, I remember having seen at Glastonbury, on a stone cross overthrown in this Queen's reign, a bronze plate on which was carved an inscription relating that Joseph of Arimathea came to Britain thirty years after Christ's passion, with eleven or twelve companions, that he was allowed by Arviragus the King to dwell at Glastonbury, which was then an island called Avalon, in a simple and solitary life: that he brought with him two small silver vessels in which was some of the most holy blood and water which flowed from the side of Christ. This cross, moreover, had been set up many years before to mark the length of the chapel of the Blessed Virgin, made by Joseph with hurdles. The length was measured by a straight line from the centre of the cross to the side of the chancel afterward built of hewn stone, under which also there was of old, in a subterranean crypt, the Chapel of St. Joseph. Outside, in the wall of this Chapel of the Blessed Virgin, there was a stone with the words *Jesus, Maria,* carved in very ancient letters.*

"There was likewise at Glastonbury, in a long subterranean chapel, a most famous place of pilgrimage which was made to a stone image of St. Joseph there, and many miracles were wrought at it. When I was a boy of eight, for I was born there, I have served Mass in this chapel."

* This inscription is still to be seen.

[75]

10

THE STONE IMAGE of Joseph of Arimathea
was by no means the only object of the pil-
grimages to Glastonbury during the last two centuries before its destruction. Relics, or supposed
relics, which were on view to the pious or the
credulous included (according to John of Glastonbury, who wrote at the end of the fourteenth
century) fragments of the bodies of Patrick and
Columba, of Martin of Tours and the Germain
who had first brought Patrick to St. Albans, of
Helena, the British mother of Constantine the
Great, of George, the Patron of England, of Illtyd
of Wales. There was a thread from the robe of
the Virgin Mary and a stone which Jesus, in the
wilderness, had refused to turn into bread, some

of the gold that the Wise Men had offered Him and a splinter from the table of the Last Supper. Nor was the Old Testament neglected. There was some manna which had fallen in the wilderness and a chip from the stone on which Jacob laid his head when he dreamt of the heavenly ladder; there was a sliver from Aaron's rod, which had so miraculously budded, and a piece of Isaiah's tomb.

From all parts of the known world, pilgrims came to Glastonbury and took the fame of the great Abbey back to their own lands. The church had become, by the rebuilding of successive Abbots, a total length of 594 feet, larger than any other in England except Old St. Paul's; the community was, in numbers and in wealth, second only to Westminster; the domain was so vast that men said that "if the Abbot of Glastonbury married the Abbess of Shrewsbury they would have more land than the King of England." The "Abbot's Kitchen," the only part of the building still intact, built at the beginning of the fourteenth century, served merely the dining-room for the pilgrims and guests and its size is eloquent of their number. The library was one of the finest in the country and when Richard Whiting, who became Abbot in 1525, showed the antiquary John Leland the illuminated manuscripts and rare parchments it contained, the treasures of a thousand years, he stood spell-bound on the threshold, "being so amazed at the sight and the wonder of it that he hesitated to enter." In scientific things, a Glastonbury monk, Peter Lightfoot, made for the Abbey a great clock like the one, constructed by his pupils, which may be seen still at Wells Cathedral—the only one to survive the Dissolution.

The dial of the clock is almost six and a half feet in diameter. At each corner of the square frame that encases it is an angel holding one of the four winds. The outer circle is divided into twenty-four parts to represent the twenty-four hours of the day and a large gilt star, representing the Sun, points to the hour as it moves round the earth. An inner, second circle shows the minutes by means of a small star which moves round it every hour. A third circle gives the days of the lunar month and a crescent shows the moon's age. Above the clock is a tower, round which knights on horseback revolve in opposite directions as the clock strikes the hour, as if they were fighting in a tournament. The strike is made by a figure called Jack Blandifer who sits a little way from the clock and higher up and hits its heels against bells. The date of the clock at Glastonbury was, probably, about 1330; that of Wells about half-a-century later.

Of all the treasures of Glastonbury, spiritual and artistic, this is not the place to speak. That is another kind of study into which researches are still proceeding. But of the effect of the power and the wealth and the fame something must be said. On the eve of the Dissolution, there may not have been—indeed there was not—conduct to give scandal; but there seems to have been a great slackening of spirituality. When the last Abbot entered on his office it was, as one Catholic historian has expressed it, "as head of a large, wealthy, respected corporation, which still paid lip-service to sanctity and scholarship, but produced neither."

It was almost natural that, when King Henry VIII expressed his wish to divorce his wife Catherine to whom he had been married for twenty-one years in order that he might marry Anne Boleyn, the Abbot of Glastonbury should sign a letter to the Pope in which with other Lords Spiritual and Lords Temporal, he urged him to grant the King's request. Again, when the Pope remained adamant, the Abbot and fifty-one Glastonbury monks signed a paper renouncing allegiance to Rome and later another recognizing Henry VIII as Head of the Church, although by this time St. Thomas More and St. John Fisher and other lesser-known men had chosen martyrdom as an alternative to that particular apostasy. Yet even this acquiescence might not have availed had not the life of the monks been beyond reproach.

In that August of 1535 when Richard Layton, collecting evidence of monkish misconduct, had arrived at Glastonbury and had sent to Court the sprig of the Holy Thorn "wrapped in black and white sarsnet," he was forced by the circumstances of the case also to report: "At Glastonbury there is nothing notable; the brethren be so strait kept that they cannot offend." Yet even the accommodation of the diplomatic Abbot combined with the probity of the monks could not in the end save Glastonbury and the Abbot himself was destined for a martyr's death.

11

I T WAS IN THE spring of 1539 that the King's
Commissioners arrived the second time at the
Abbey. They were in the process of collecting
from the larger churches of the country any plate
that might be considered superfluous. In this cate-
gory they included and took away for the Royal
coffers, among other things, the great "superaltar
garnished with silver gilt and part gold, called the
Great Sapphire of Glastonbury" which had es-
caped the Danish pillage five hundred years before. The final pillage was now only a matter of
time. The King's Treasury was empty and the three
remaining Abbeys, Colchester, Reading and, more
particularly, Glastonbury were obviously destined
to replenish them. Thomas Cromwell made a

note in his memorandum-book: "Proceed against the Abbots of Reading, Glaston and the other, in their own countries."

Richard Layton, accompanied by other Commissioners, arrived early in the morning of Friday, September 19, 1539. The Abbot, Richard Whiting, now eighty years old, was at his grange a mile away. Now that events had clarified the choice that faced him, all compromise had gone. He was a simple monk again, seeing with simplicity. A century and a half after his death, tradition pointed out among the ruins of his house, his bed. It was "without tester or post, was boarded at bottom, and had a board nailed shelving at the head." "I was desired," writes the visitor who describes it, "to observe it as a curiosity." On this Gasquet, the Abbot's biographer, comments: "The existence of the tradition is proof at least, of an abiding belief on the spot, in the simplicity of life of the last lord of that glorious monastery."

To the simple grange, the Commissioners hurried, arrested the Abbot, searched his rooms in the Abbey itself where they discovered a manuscript "in favour of Queen Catherine and against the marriage of Queen Anne" and sent him, guarded, to the Tower of London. Here he was secretly examined by Thomas Cromwell, who duly noted: "Councillors to give evidence against the Abbot of Glaston. . . *Item* To see that the

"The owl of evening and the woodland fox
For their abode the shrines of Waltham choose;
Proud Glastonbury can no more refuse
To stoop her head behind these desperate shocks—"

evidence be well sorted and the indictment well drawn. . . *Item* The Abbot of Glaston to be tried at Glaston and executed there." There was to be no doubt about the verdict in the trial. Legally, the Abbot should have been tried by Parliament, as he was a member of the House of Lords; but Cromwell made haste to send him back to Somerset where, before a carefully picked jury, he was sentenced to death for treason.

The martyrdom of the last Abbot of Glastonbury was one of the horrors even of that time. The old man was stretched on a hurdle and dragged not only through the town, but up to the top of the Tor where a gibbet had been erected by St. Michael's Chapel. This terrible, unnecessary journey does indeed bring a sense of darkness as if suddenly the old gods had returned to their dwelling-place to savor of human sacrifice.

They set the Abbot's head over the gate of the Abbey while the pillage proceeded. Everything, including the lead of the roof, was stripped. Books and vestments were auctioned to the highest bidder; but most of the spoils were saved for the Royal Treasury. To quote Cromwell's memoranda again: "The plate of Glastonbury, 11,000 ounces and over, besides golden. The furniture of the house of Glaston. In ready money from Glaston, £11,000 and over. The rich copes from Glaston. The whole year's revenue of Glaston." The prop-

erty itself was sold or given to those gentlemen
who had helped the King, including the steward
of the Abbey, John Horner. He was given the
manor of Mells, and lives still in traditional rhyme:

> Little Jack Horner
> Sat in the corner,
> Eating a Christmas Pie;
> He put in his thumb
> And pulled out a plum,
> And said, What a good boy am I.

That Christmas was, indeed, except for Horner
and his like, a time of desolation. Wordsworth
has memorialized it:

Threats come which no submission may assuage;
No sacrifice avert, no power dispute;
The tapers shall be quenched, the belfries mute,
And 'mid their choirs unroofed by selfish rage,
The warbling wren shall find a leafy cage;
The gadding bramble hang her purple fruit;
And the green lizard and the gilded newt
Lead unmolested lives and die of age.
The owl of evening and the woodland fox
For their abode the shrines of Waltham choose;
Proud Glastonbury can no more refuse
To stoop her head behind these desperate shocks—
She whose high pomp displaced, as story tells,
Arimathean Joseph's wattled cells.

But the Hawthorn still flowered on Weary-all
Hill.

12

THIS CONTINUED FLOWERING became an of-
fense to the Puritans and in the reign of
Elizabeth I a local zealot determined to hack the
tree down. Ascending the Hill with his hatchet,
he managed to fell the larger of the trunks, all but
a sliver, but when he started on the smaller trunk
a chip flew into his eye and blinded it. To the
general satisfaction of the spectators, he aban-
doned the attempt and the hawthorn continued
to flower. More and more spectators were at-
tracted to it and its fame spread. Merchants from
Bristol took cuttings and sold them abroad. King
James I paid a considerable sum for one; and the
Bishop of Bath and Wells presented his Queen
at Christmastide with blossoms from the original

stem. The custom continued and, in the reign of their son Charles I, gave rise to a story which the Queen's confessor, Père Cyprian Gamache, was fond of repeating.

"Well," said the King, holding out his hand one Christmas Day to take the flowering branch, "this is a miracle, is it?"

"Yes, Your Majesty," replied the officer who presented it, "a miracle peculiar to England and regarded with great veneration by the Catholics."

"How?" said the King, "when this miracle opposes itself to the Pope?"

Everyone in the Royal circle, Papist and Protestant alike, looked astonished.

"You bring me this miraculous branch on Christmas Day, Old Style. Does it always observe the Old Style, by which we English celebrate the Nativity, in its time of flowering?", asked Charles.

"Always," replied the officer.

"Then," said the King, "the Pope and your miracle differ not a little, for he always celebrates Christmas Day ten days earlier by the calendar of the New Style, which has been ordained at Rome by papal orders for nearly a century."

The revision of the calendar, which since the days of Julius Caesar had gradually diverged from the solar year, had been brought into line with it by Pope Gregory XIII in 1582. Unfortunately, the theological bitterness of the time made the

". . . but when he started on the smaller trunk a chip
flew into his eye and blinded it."

Protestant countries refuse to co-operate with the Pope even on a matter of chronological accuracy, so that, when the Catholic countries righted the discrepancy by cutting ten days out of the year—in 1582, October 15 followed immediately on October 4—England continued to hold to the old style of dating. It was not until 1751, by which time the discrepancy between the sun and the calendar had increased, that "Chesterfield's Act" brought England into line with the Continent by decreeing that September 2, 1752, should be immediately followed by September 14.

In that year there was, inevitably, widespread interest in how the Holy Thorn would react to the change. According to the *Somerset Evening Post* at the beginning of 1753: "A vast concourse of people attended the noted Thorn on Christmas Day, New Style, but to their great disappointment there was no appearance of its blowing, which made them watch it narrowly the 6 January, the Christmas Day, Old Style, when it blowed as usual."

It will be remembered that January 6, the Feast of the Epiphany, was in fact observed as Christmas Day in the time of Joseph of Arimathea and for three centuries afterwards, so the Thorn can hardly be accused of inconsistency. One wonders how far Charles I was aware of this.

It was shortly after his execution that the Puri-

tans, now triumphant under another Cromwell—
Oliver—decided that the remaining trunk of the
Thorn must be cut down. This time it was accomplished without any injury to the executioner,
though not altogether without protest. Bishop
Goodman wrote to Oliver Cromwell in 1653:
"The White Thorn at Glastonbury which did
usually blossom on Christmas Day was cut down;
yet I did not hear that the party was punished.
Certainly the Thorn was very extraordinary, for
at my being there I did consider the place, how
it was sheltered: I did consider the soil and all
other circumstances; yet I could find no natural
cause. This I know, that God first appeared to
Moses in a bramble-bush, and that Aaron's Rod,
being dried and withered, did bud; and as these
were God's actions and His first actions; and truly,
Glastonbury was a place noted for holiness and
the first religious foundation in England; and, in
effect, was the first dissolved and therein was
such a barbarous inhumanity as Egypt never heard
the like, it may well be that this White Thorn did
spring up and begin to blossom on Christmas Day
to give a testimony to religion that it doth flourish
in persecution; as the Thorn doth flourish in the
coldest time of winter, so religion should stand,
or rather, rise up though religious houses were
pulled down."

So complete was the obliteration of Glastonbury

that, in the intervening century between the Bishop's writing and the pillage, it seems that the very name of Joseph of Arimathea had been temporarily forgotten. And at the Restoration, the Thorn had become, for one of the wits merely a proverbial term of reference. Sir Charles Sedley wrote:

> Cornelia's charms inspire my lays
> Who fair in nature's scorn
> Blooms in the winter of her days
> Like Glastonbury's Thorn.

But Joseph of Arimathea was to return again, this time in an indubitably inaccurate manner. When the change of the calendar took place, a stump of the original thorn was still left. By the end of the eighteenth century it had disappeared —cut down at last, but not, of course, before there were other thorns budded from it—and where it had stood, a John Clark had put a monumental slab with the inscription: "J.A. Anno D. XXXI." The "J.A." is obviously Joseph of Arimathea; but the date 31 A.D., which is before the Crucifixion, is the result of a misreading of the bronze tablet which, in the Middle Ages, had been fixed to a column in the great church. This stated: "In the year XXXI after the Lord's Passion, twelve holy men, of whom Joseph of Arimathea was the chief, came hither and built the first church of this kingdom, in this place which Christ at this time dedicated to the honour of His Mother and as a place for their burial." Thirty-one years after the Lord's Passion was the year 63/64 A.D., which had always been the traditional date for Joseph's visit.

Glastonbury fell into increasing desolation as the centuries passed. One of its owners in the eighteenth century was a Puritan who took a perverse delight in heaping-up great Guy Fawkes Day bonfires against the Lady Chapel (the marks may still be seen on the stones) and saw to it, according to a visitor, that "there was more barbarous havoc there than had been since the Dissolution; for every week a pillar or buttress, a window jamb or an angle of fine hewn stone is sold to the best bidder. Whilst I was there they were excoriating St. Joseph's Chapel for that purpose, and the squared stones were laid up by lots in the Abbot's Kitchen; the rest goes to paving yards and stalls for cattle, or to the highway."

The Abbey continued in private hands until, in 1908 a fund was started, to which the King, the Queen and the Prince of Wales (afterwards King George V) subscribed to buy it for the Church of England; and the following year the title deeds were handed over to the Archbishop of Canterbury. Slowly order and decency were restored and excavations were started to establish various sites in the Abbey.

Among the many discoveries, one in particular deserves mention, not only because it has an air of mystery about it, but because it takes us back to the earliest stories. It was a terra-cotta medallion. On one side was a cross and the sacred monogram IHS. On the other, the date 1105 in Roman numerals, MCV. Above the M and V are stars (which draw immediate attention to the Virgin Mary), and above them a hand held out in blessing. In the centre of the hand is a small indentation which suggests that it originally held a jewel. What does it mean?

In 1105, the Abbot who was the predecessor of the great Henry of Blois had started to build a new church. That era was also the time of considerable devotion to St. David, who was actually canonized in 1120. St. David, it will be remembered, had himself come to Glastonbury to dedicate a church to the Blessed Virgin but was shown in a vision that the Old Church was already hers, and in consequence built another church a little distance away. In this vision, Christ, as a token of the truth of it, laid his finger on the palm of David's right hand and inflicted there a small wound. He promised that when David, at his Mass the next morning, reached the end of the Canon and with the words "per ipsum et cum ipso and in ipso" (through Him and with Him and in Him) made the final sign of the cross over the consecrated elements, the wound would disappear. This David proved and, in obedience, made no attempt to consecrate Joseph of Arimathea's original church but started building a small one of his own.

It seems, therefore, probable that some small red stone was originally in the indentation of the hand and that it was a memorial at what may have been the rebuilding of St. David's church that there could never be any attempt to supersede, however magnificent the structure, Joseph's original church dedicated to the Virgin Mary by the command of her Son Himself.

And the flowering Hawthorn? Though the original Thorn has gone and the slab may have something of the appearance of a tombstone, many thorns have been budded from the parent stem. At Glastonbury one can be seen in the Abbey grounds; there is a better one in the churchyard of the parish church (on whose altar blossoms are put every Christmastide); and a better one still in the Vicarage garden.

The destroyers did not destroy and though, "far away in the western shires"—the sentence is Chesterton's—they "cut down the Thorn of Glastonbury, from which had grown the whole story

". . . a hand held out in blessing."

of Britain," it did not cease to flower any more than the story of Britain ceased to unfold.

The unfolding was to more than the little island in the mists at the edge of the world. As once Joseph's journey was made possible by the roads Rome had made in Europe, so a later empire was to make seaways to the wider world to carry its lore and its language. To America, to the African Cape, to Australia to New Zealand, it spread as England expanded into the English-speaking community. And to all of it, continents and islands, Glastonbury by right belongs as the gate by which Christianity entered. America, in particular, must have known the Thorn itself, for the Bristol traders are known to have taken cuttings of it on their journeys.

And as, from the ruins of the "holiest earth in England," it went out into the unimagined future, so it became a pilgrim-witness to its past—to the unexampled splendor of the Abbey which was the "second Rome" and to the learning of the Middle Ages; to the statesmen, Dunstan and Henry of Blois, who forged a state from antagonistic elements, and to the great soldiers who saved faith and order from engulfing chaos and made themselves legends for ever—Alfred and Arthur; to the saints who are still the patrons of Ireland and Wales, Patrick and David, and to the first founder

[101]

who came from Arimathea to the Isle of Avalon where immemorially the shades of a strange religion darkened the hill-top.

And, in the end, to a tree on another hill, outside the gates of Jerusalem.

THE AUTHOR, THE
ILLUSTRATOR, AND THEIR
BOOK

HUGH ROSS WILLIAMSON, *historian, theologian, playwright and novelist, was born January 2, 1901 in the town of Romsey, Hampshire, England. He was graduated in 1922 from the University of London, with a B.A. Honors degree in history, a subject which he has utilized in most of his writings. He taught school for a short time and in 1925 joined the editorial staff of the Yorkshire Post. Later he became drama critic for that newspaper. He has written a dozen plays since 1927. Unable to serve in World War II because of lameness, he turned to the Church of England, being a member of the clergy from 1943 to 1955, when he became a convert to Catholicism. He is married to the former Margaret Joan Cox, a scientist who is a television producer in the Schools Department of the BBC; they have two children, Julia and Hugh, and make their home in London. A frequent contributor to the British networks, Mr. Williamson has also appeared in most of Britain's scholarly and popular magazines. Among his books are:* The Poetry of T. S. Eliot *(Hodder and Stoughton, 1932; Putnam's, 1933);* John Hampden *(Hodder and Stoughton, 1933);* Gods and Mortals in Love *(Country Life, 1935);* King James I *(Duckworth, 1935);* Who is for Liberty? *(Michael Joseph, 1939);* George Villiers, First Duke of Buckingham *(Duckworth, 1940);* A.D. 33 *(Collins, 1941);* Captain Thomas Schofield *(Collins, 1942);* Charles and Cromwell *(Duckworth, 1946);* The Story Without an End *(Mowbray, 1947; Morehouse, 1947);* Were You There? *(Mowbray, 1947);* The Arrow and the Sword *(Faber and Faber, 1947);* The Silver Bowl *(Michael Joseph, 1948);* Four Stuart Portraits *(Evans, 1949);* Sir Walter Raleigh *(Faber and Faber, 1951);* The Gunpowder Plot *(Faber and Faber, 1951);* The Seven Christian Virtues *(SCM Press, 1951);* Jeremy Taylor *(Dobson, 1952);* The Ancient Capital *(Muller, 1953);* Canterbury Cathedral *(Country Life, 1953; Transatlantic, 1953);* The Children's Book of British Saints *(Harrap, 1953);* The Children's Book of French Saints *(Harrap, 1954);* The Children's Book of Italian Saints *(Harrap, 1955);* The Great Prayer *(Collins, 1955; Macmillan, 1955);* Historical Whodunits *(Phoenix House, 1955; Macmillan, 1955);* James, By the Grace of God—*(Michael Joseph, 1955; Regnery, 1956);* The Children's Book of Spanish Saints *(Harrap, 1956);* The Walled Garden *(Autobiography; Michael Joseph, 1956; Macmillan, 1957);* Enigmas of History *(Michael Joseph, 1957); Macmillan, 1957);* The Day They Killed the King *(Muller, 1957; Macmillan, 1957);* The Beginning of the English Reformation *(Sheed and Ward, 1957);* The Mime of Bernadette *(Burns Oates & Washbourne, 1958);* The Challenge of Bernadette *(Burns Oates & Washbourne, 1958; Newman Press, 1958);* The Children's Book of German Saints *(Harrap, 1958);* The Conspirators and the Crown *(Hawthorn, 1959);* The Young People's Book of Saints *(Hawthorn, 1960); and* A Wicked Pack of Cards *(Joseph, 1961).*

CLARE LEIGHTON, *illustrator and author, was born in London in 1901. She attended the Brighton School of Art and Slade School and received the honorary degree of Doctor of Fine Arts from Colby College. She was elected to the Society of Wood Engravers in 1928 and received first prize in the International Engraving Exhibition at the Art Institute of Chicago in 1930. She is a fellow in the Royal Society of Painters, Etchers and Engravers and has been vice-president of both the National Academy of Design and the National Institute of Arts and Letters. Presently, she resides in Woodbury, Connecticut. She has illustrated innumerable works, both classic and contemporary. Books both written and illustrated by Miss Leighton include* Sometime-Never *(Macmillan, 1939),* Give Us This Day *(Reynal & Hitchcock, 1943),* Tempestuous Petticoat *(Rinehart, 1947), and* Where Land Meets Sea: The Tideline of Cape Cod *(Holt, Rinehart & Winston, 1954).*

THE FLOWERING HAWTHORN *(Hawthorn Books, 1962) was designed by Sidney Feinberg. It was set in type and printed by Hamilton Printing Company, Rensselaer, N. Y., and was bound by Montauk Book Manufacturing Co., Inc., New York, N. Y. The body type was set on the Linotype in Times Roman, originally designed for use by* The Times *of London.*

A HAWTHORN BOOK